How Farming Has Changed

Bethany Daniels

INFOMAX COMMON CORE READERS

Rosen Classroom™

New York

Published in 2014 by The Rosen Publishing Group, Inc.
29 East 21st Street, New York, NY 10010

Book Design: Mickey Harmon

Photo Credits: Cover MaxyM/Shutterstock.com; p. 5 Tim Roberts Photography/Shutterstock.com; p. 7 Dervin Witmer/Shutterstock.com; p. 9 Sunny Forest/Shutterstock.com; p. 11 Edouard Debat-Ponsan/The Bridgeman Art Library/Getty Images; p. 13 Tom Murphy VII/Wikipedia.org; p. 15 Domofon/Shutterstock.com; p. 17 Valio/Shutterstock.com; p. 19 Todd Klassy/Shutterstock.com; p. 21 BMJ/Shutterstock.com; p. 22 Dudarev Mikhail/Shutterstock.com.

ISBN: 978-1-4777-2404-0
6-pack ISBN: 978-1-4777-2405-7

Manufactured in the United States of America

CPSIA Compliance Information: Batch #CS13RC: For further information contact Rosen Publishing, New York, New York at 1-800-237-9932.

Contents

American Agriculture

There are a lot of farms in America. You may have visited one before, or your family may even live on a farm!

Farming, or agriculture (AA-grih-kuhl-chur), has always been important to Americans. It's changed a lot over the years. The invention of machines, rise of cities, and need for foods have shaped the role of farming in America.

American soil is good for farming. This is one reason why farming has been such a big part of our country's history.

The History of Farming

A long time ago, people had to grow food for themselves. They didn't have grocery stores like we do today.

Many early Americans felt the best way to make a living was to run a farm. They moved to areas with more land so they could grow crops and raise animals. Many of these farms were far from the cities.

Many Americans moved to states in the middle of the country, where they could get a lot of land to run big farms.

America's **population** grew, which meant more food was needed. However, people in towns and cities didn't grow their own food. Much like today, they depended on farmers. Soon, farming became a common job.

Farmers worked hard and had many **responsibilities**. They had to get up early in the morning, often before sunrise! They worked outside all day, caring for crops and animals.

Early morning farm duties included feeding animals, milking cows, and working outside before it got too hot to work.

In the past, farmers did everything by hand. The tools they used were simple. Most were made of wood and a little metal. One example is the plow.

Farmers used plows to break up the land so they could plant crops. The plows were very heavy. Sometimes it took four or five oxen to pull one! It wasn't easy to till the land this way. Usually, farmers could only till a small area each day.

Farmers pushed the plow while oxen pulled it. It was a very tiring task.

The Cotton Gin

Because tools were so simple, it took farmers a long time to finish their work. They also got tired quickly. Soon, inventors started thinking of ways to make farming easier.

In 1793, a man named Eli Whitney invented the cotton gin. Before this machine, picking cotton was hard and took a long time. The cotton gin made it faster and easier. It saved farmers money, too. It changed farming forever.

This shows how the cotton gin worked. Its hooks separated seeds from the cotton. Brushes moved the loose cotton to keep the machine from getting stuck.

Whitney's Great Invention

1. Cotton with seeds goes into machine.
2. Cylinder turns and pulls cotton through a comb-like grid.
3. Hooks in grid separate cotton from its seeds.
4. Brushes sweep clean cotton off grid and to end of machine.

The cotton gin showed how machines could improve a farmer's tasks. Farmers now wanted machines to do some of the work for them. So, inventors created machines to help with tasks such as **harvesting** grain and cutting down crops.

Another big change came when people made tools out of steel instead of wood. Steel tools lasted longer and didn't break as often. They made farmwork easier, too.

Having better tools helped farmers a lot!

Farming Begins to Change

By the 1860s, almost half of Americans were farmers. It stayed this way until the early 1900s when people began looking for work in cities.

Over time, new farm **equipment** allowed farmers to work more land. They also chose to work with only one or two major crops. This was the beginning of modern agriculture.

Today, there are fewer farmers than there were long ago. Most Americans work in cities.

Farming Today

Today, a farmer's job is very different from what it was long ago. The biggest difference is the use of advanced machines to help with the work.

Farmers use machines such as tractors and crop dusters to help cover large amounts of land quickly. They also use fertilizers (FUHR-tuh-ly-zuhrz) and insecticides (ihn-SEHK-tuh-sydz) to grow healthy crops. These things solved some of the worst problems farmers faced long ago.

Fertilizers help farmers grow healthy plants. Insecticides keep plants safe from bugs.

Farms today are less **diverse** than they used to be. In the past, farms grew and raised many things to give people everything they needed. Today, many farmers focus on growing only one kind of crop or raising one kind of animal.

Today, you'll find farms that only grow corn or soybeans. Some farms grow fruit, and others only grow lettuce and other vegetables. There are also farms that raise just pigs or cattle.

Today, farmers use refrigerated trucks and trains to send their crops to faraway places. This allows them to focus on only one or two things.

Thanking Our Farmers

Modern farming is different from the way it was long ago. However, farming would not be what it is today without the changes that happened over the last two hundred years.

Without farmers, we wouldn't have fruits, vegetables, or meat. We also wouldn't have plants we use to make clothes and other things we use in our daily lives. We have these things thanks to our farmers!

Glossary

diverse (dih-VUHRS) Of different kinds or sorts.

equipment (ih-KWIHP-muhnt) The tools needed for a certain purpose.

harvest (HAHR-vuhst) The process of gathering crops.

population (pah-pyuh-LAY-shun) The number of people who live somewhere.

responsibility (rih-spahn-suh-BIH-luh-tee) A duty or task that you have to do.

Index